# Home on
# THE PRAIRIE

Written by Neil and Ting Morris
Illustrated by Anna Clarke
Historical advisor: Marion Wood

Evans

Evans Brothers Limited

Published by Evans Brothers Limited
2A Portman Mansions, Chiltern Street
London W1M 1LE

First published 1988

Printed in Hong Kong by Wing King Tong Co. Ltd.

ISBN 0 237 50973 3

# INTRODUCTION

A new nation was born in 1783 when the Revolutionary War ended and the United States gained independence. At that time the western boundary was formed by the Mississippi River. Beyond that was a vast wilderness, the home of wild animals and nomadic tribes of Plains Indians.

In 1803 the United States made the Louisiana Purchase, buying over 2 million square kilometres of land from the French. For an agreed sum of 15 million dollars, this deal more than doubled the territory of the previous 17 states of the young republic. The new land stretched westwards from the Mississippi to the Rocky Mountains. Soon daring pioneers and fur trappers started forging trails into the forests, mountains and deserts of this unmapped new territory.

In 1862 the US Congress passed the Homestead Act. This law allowed any adult to have 160 acres of land if they put up their own house and produced a crop within five years. The settlers who came west to take up land did not see themselves as taking territory from the Indians: they came to find good farming land. At first the settlers used sod or turf as building material, but when they could afford or find the wood, they built more substantial log cabins. The new railroads opened up the West and attracted even more people to settle on the prairies.

This is the story of one family of settlers, and their adventures on the prairie. The information pages with the rifle border will tell you more about the life and work of the settlers of the American West.

After weeks of travelling, father stopped the wagon. 'This is our new home,' he said. 'But where is the house?' the girls asked. 'We'll build it right here,' father told them. 'Why not closer to the river?' asked Tom. 'Because this is Indian country and we don't want enemies,' his mother said.

The girls quickly felt at home. 'Look at the flowers we picked for you,' Rosy said when her mother came back with water. 'There's no one at the creek,' she told her husband. But Tom had found Indian tracks. 'Can't trust the Indians,' he said. '*I'll* go for water from now on.'

# Homes

There were few trees on the prairie, so the settlers used sod or turf as building material. The sod blocks were built up like a brick wall. Door and window frames were made from packing cases. Cracks were filled in with mud.

Some made their homes in dug-outs. They dug a cave into the side of a hill so that only a front wall needed to be built.

Shanties were made of rough boards and had tar paper roofs, but they were hot in summer and draughty in winter. Settlers piled earth against the outside wall to keep warm.

As soon as the family could afford the wood, they built a log cabin with a wooden floor. The settlers' houses had no plumbing, and the lavatory was in an outhouse.

Soon they planted their first crops. But one day when they were ploughing, their last blade broke. 'I've talked it over with your mother,' father said. 'We're out of money. I'll take a job at the railroad and be back for harvest time.'

Tom begged his father to let him come. 'Two of us stand a better chance of getting a job,' he said. 'Mother and the girls will be safe on their own. I've kept a look-out and there are no new Indian tracks. They've gone for good.'

Tom had finally got his way. He and his father were hired
as track-layers, but it was hard and dangerous work. The
crew worked in constant danger of attack by Indians. The
tribes feared the 'iron horse' spreading across their land. It
was an all-out war for survival.

# Railroads

The Central Pacific woodburning locomotive, Jupiter. In 1862 two companies built a railroad between the Missouri River and the Pacific coast. This railroad opened up the Far West and attracted more people to settle on the prairie. The Central Pacific track was built eastward from Sacramento, and the Union Pacific track westward. The two lines followed the California trail and met up in May 1869.

Building a railroad was hard work. Chinese coolies laid most of the tracks for the Central Pacific. To blast a way through the sides of the mountains, men were lowered in baskets. For blasting, black gunpowder was fired from close up. The men only had handtools, picks, shovels and saws. Often the track-laying crew worked in danger of Indian attacks. The tribes feared that the 'iron horse' would bring more buffalo hunters and settlers into their territory.

Tom was posted as a look-out, and every day he saw
hundreds of buffalo killed. This gave meat to the railway
workers, but most of the animals were left to rot. There
were times when Tom could understand the Indians' anger.

One night Indian warriors attacked. When they had been
beaten off, Tom's father told him he must go home. 'There
have been massacres all over the plains. You must go and
look after your mother and sisters,' he said.

Tom knew his father was right. He had never seen so many
Indians on the war path. He left at once and got the
stage-coach at the nearest stopping place to speed up the
journey.

'Not long now,' Tom thought. Suddenly two masked riders appeared. 'Throw down the box!' a voice shouted. The driver unchained the strongbox, as Tom pulled the trigger. His bullets hit the bandits. 'Tie them up and take them to the sheriff,' Tom said. 'I'll take the horses as my reward!'

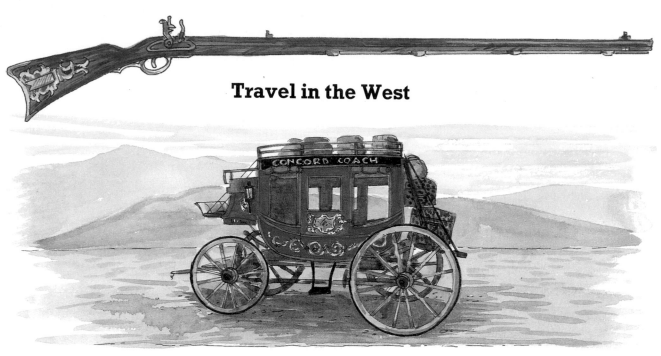

# Travel in the West

Before the railroads spread across the West, the stage-coach carried passengers, mail and valuables. One of the most famous stage-coaches was the Concord. It carried up to 14 passengers, with room for their luggage and a strongbox for valuables. Shotgun guards usually went along to protect the coach against bandits and Indian attacks. The biggest stage-coach line was run by the Wells Fargo company.

The fastest mail service – 13 days from East to West – was run by relays of pony express riders. They used the California trail and changed their ponies three times at relay stations along the route. Pony express riders were boys chosen for their lightness, speed and fearlessness. The pony express service only lasted 18 months. Once the telegraph lines were opened, messages could travel in morse code in a few minutes.

Tom rode as fast as he could. But when he reached the creek near home, he saw a new trail and then . . . tipis . . . many tipis and Indian braves, women and children. Tom felt really scared. Were his mother and sisters still alive?

He rode on, through the fields where the wheat was now growing high. And there was the little house. He shivered when he saw two Indians leaving. What had they done to his family?

'Mother, thank heavens you are all right,' Tom cried. 'We are fine, Tom,' his mother said. 'The Indians didn't harm us, they gave us water in exchange for my cornbread and some of father's tobacco. But now we have run out of everything and there is no more water.'

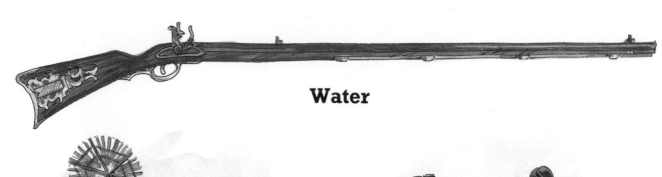

# Water

The settlers often dug a well near their sod house or log cabin, and hauled water up in buckets.

Sometimes the water was very deep under ground, and farmers built windmills to haul up the water. To find water, a so-called 'water witch' used a Y-shaped willow switch. When the switch moved, it meant that water lay directly below.

Where there were rivers, settlers dug ditches and built wooden sluiceways to bring water down to their farms.

Tom promised his mother that from now on they would
have their own water. Early next day he started digging a
well. 'More rope!' he shouted from the deep pit, and then,
'Water!' 'It's the best water I've ever tasted,' Rosy said.

They were all so excited that they hardly noticed the
terrible heat that was growing and growing. Then Tom
saw a wall of flames moving across the open plains
towards them.

They were saved by a torrential rain storm. Water came
pouring through all the cracks and the roof. 'Get under the
table,' mother shouted as the roof came crashing down.
Luckily no one was hurt. 'We'll build a stronger and better
house next time,' Tom told his sisters.

'All our work has been destroyed,' Tom said to his mother. 'The crops father planted, the house you made our home.' 'But we are all well, Tom, and that's what matters most,' she said. 'It's harvest time and father will be back soon.'

Tom ran down to the creek. The tipis had gone, the Indians had moved on. He looked around at the trees. 'We could build a log cabin,' he thought. 'This is Indian country.' His mother's words came back to him.

'But it's our country too,' Tom thought as he ran back. There was a wagon outside their broken home, loaded with timber. His father was back. 'There won't be much harvesting,' father said, 'so let's start the house. I brought plenty of wood.' 'And there's more by the creek,' Tom said.

# Farming tools

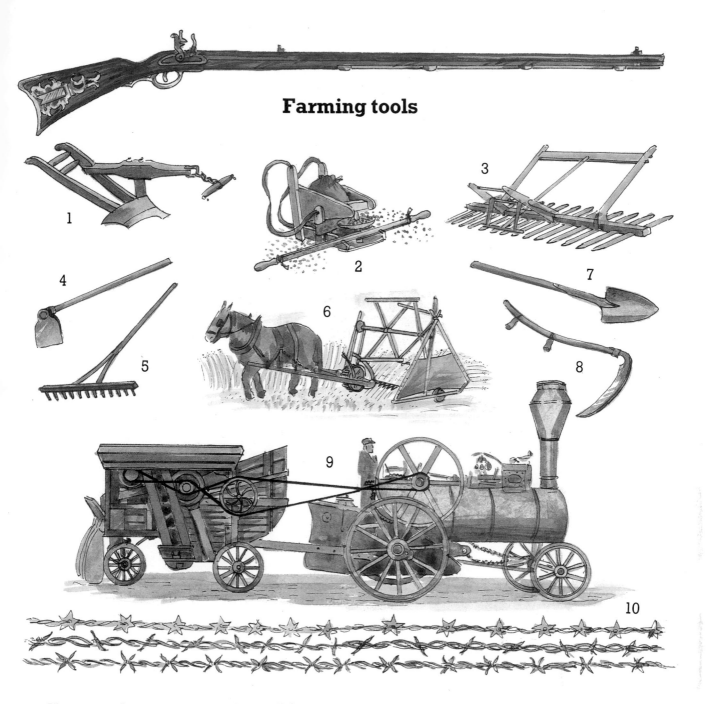

Horses and oxen were used to pull farm machines, and later steam engines were introduced.

1 pioneer plough; 2 seed fiddle; it was claimed that a sower with a fiddle could sow up to four acres an hour; 3 hay rake; 4 hoe; 5 rake; 6 reaper; 7 spade; 8 scythe; 9 thresher powered by steam engine; 10 barbed wire; its use helped hardworking settlers to farm the land without fear of longhorn trampling their crops.

Within a few days they moved into the new log cabin.
'When will our beds be ready?' the girls asked. 'At
bedtime,' father said. 'And remember, whatever you dream
on your first night will come true.' For Tom their dream had
already come true – a real home on the prairie.

This map of the American West shows the railroad and stage coach routes which the settlers used to travel West.

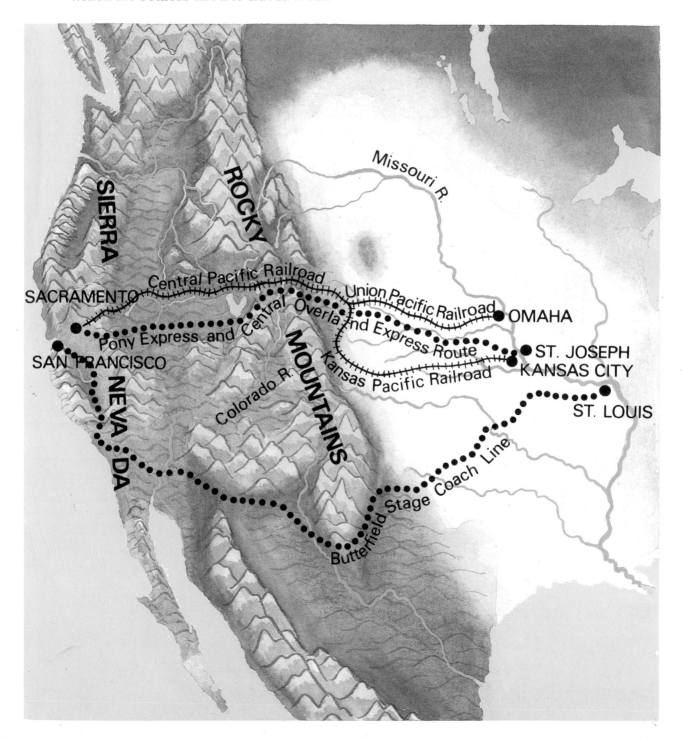